# WICCA FO

## A guide to Witchcraft for beginners: Explore Wiccan Beliefs, Wiccan Rituals, Wiccan Spells and Wiccan Magic

Wicca for beginners was created as an entry point to provide informative information to enable you to start your journey into the magical world of Wicca. The interest in Wicca is growing exponentially as more people have access to reliable information and start to realise the importance of nature based religions. This book is designed to help you grow spiritually, magically, while uncovering common misconceptions. By the end of the book you should have a good understanding of the principles of Wicca and hopefully a strong desire to continue your journey into Wicca

## WARNING

This book is designed to provide information on wiccan only. This information is provided and sold with the knowledge that the publisher and author do not offer any legal or other professional advice. In the case of a need for any such expertise consult with the appropriate professional. This book does not contain all information available on the subject. This book has not been created to be specific to any individual's or organizations' situation or needs. Every effort has been made to make this book as accurate as possible. However, there may be typographical and or content errors. Therefore, this book should serve only as a general guide and not as the ultimate source of subject information. This book contains information that might be dated and is intended only to educate and entertain. The author and publisher shall have no liability or responsibility to any person or entity regarding any loss or damage incurred, or alleged to have incurred, directly or indirectly, by the information contained in this book. You hereby agree to be bound by this disclaimer or you may return this book within the guarantee time period for a full refund.

Copyright © 2015 by

All rights reserved. No part of this publication may be reproduced, distributed, or transmitted in any form or by any means, including photocopying, recording, or other electronic or mechanical methods, without the prior written permission of the publisher, except in the case of brief quotations embodied in critical reviews and certain other noncommercial uses permitted by copyright law.

# CONTENTS

## CHAPTER ONE: Wicca, The Mystery Religion
Is Every Witch a Wiccan?...................................................8
What is Magic?................................................................ 10

## CHAPTER TWO: A Brief History of Wicca
The Persecution of Witches............................................ 16

## CHAPTER THREE: Basic Wiccan Beliefs ........
THEOLOGY ..................................................................... 22
The Elements.................................................................. 22
The Goddess and God .................................................... 25
Misconceptions .............................................................. 27

## CHAPTER FOUR: How to Practice
Casting a Circle .............................................................. 32
Spellcraft......................................................................... 35

## CHAPTER FIVE: Tools and Altars
What is an Altar and Do I Need One?............................ 42
Additional Tools ............................................................. 46

## CHAPTER SIX: Types of Magic

Herbal Magic ..................................................... 50

Cooking............................................................. 60

Potions.............................................................. 62

Candle Magic .................................................... 64

## CHAPTER SEVEN: Types of Practice

Solitary versus Coven Practice........................... 70

## CHAPTER EIGHT: The Wiccan Festivals

Sabbats ............................................................. 76

Esbats ............................................................... 81

## CHAPTER NINE: Book of Shadows

What is a Book of Shadows? ............................. 86

What Should I Include in My Own Book of Shadows? 87

## CHAPTER TEN: Divination

Runes ................................................................ 92

## A Closing Note ............................ 105

# CHAPTER ONE:
# Wicca, The Mystery Religion

# CHAPTER ONE: Wicca, The Mystery Religion

WHAT IS WICCA

## *Is Every Witch a Wiccan?*

Known as a *mystery religion,* Wicca is a nature based, all-inclusive religion that is founded upon the basic principles of balance. Balance of nature. Balance of heart and mind. Balance of man and woman. But if it's all about balance, then what's all this mystery stuff about? And what about *witchcraft* – isn't that the same thing?

First, the reason that Wicca is considered a mystery religion is because much of its practice was steeped in secrecy. Today, a lot of that has changed. Wicca is more accessible, thanks largely to things like the internet, but also because people have grown and changed as a society. Wicca is no longer quick and dirty labeled as "devil worship". Because it's not. In fact, there is no devil in the Wiccan religion. It's a very Christian concept, meaning to worship it, you would have to in some way acknowledge the theology of Christianity.

All of which is fine, but has little to do with Wicca.

Once upon a time, the secrecy that shrouded Wicca – and all types of paganism and witchcraft – protected those that practiced it. It saved people's lives, protected them from the persecution of those that could not understand. In an era where anything that wasn't Christian – in some form or another – was considered wicked and damned, it was imperative that those who partook in the "mystery religions" (pagan traditions) hide their traditions, their worship, and their beliefs from the outside world.

But back to what Wicca *is* (we'll get back to the persecution later on).

The important part of this is "religion". When people think Wicca, they think witch, and while it's true that every Wiccan could be considered a type of witch, the reverse is not true. Not every witch will also be a Wiccan. For instance, you could be a Druid, a Voodoo practitioner, a Pagan, or merely what's deemed "eclectic". All of these religions constitute a type of magic practice that will likely get you called a witch, but they're not all the same.

In the end, the defining factor between Wiccan and witch is relatively simple: A witch is one who practices magic. A Wiccan is one who follows the religious beliefs of Wicca and uses magic like prayer.

Magic is still part of the mix, but Wicca is more specific about how to do that magic and what its purpose is. And ultimately, if you wanted to cut out the "magic" part altogether, you could.

### What is Magic?

But before we go any further, let's talk about what magic really is.

Magic is like a will. It's an invisible force that drives. Magic has no specific alignment, neither good nor evil. It simply is, the same way an inanimate object – say your favorite pillow – is not good or evil. We can associate good or bad things with your pillow, but that does not make your pillow those things. A pillow, in the end, is just a pillow.

Instead, magic becomes good or evil based on the person wielding it. Think of a sword. A sword is sharp, even deadly – but it's just a sword. Until you give it to a crazy ninth century Viking. Now it's a weapon and heading for the hills seems like a *great* idea.

So, we've established that magic is the equivalent of neutral, taking on the characteristics of its wielder. But that still doesn't really tell us what magic *is*.

It is an invisible force, a will, that affects the world around us. Usually when we think of magic, we think of wiggling our noses and POP the living room is clean. Or we think of Harry Potter waving a wand to change his goblet into a toad. But magic is a lot more complicated than that and in the end, a lot less *noticeable*. Magic can affect the world around us, but it works in subtle ways. It shows up in very mundane ways, but which happen to fit our specifications of the spell cast.

I'll give you a quick example of this.

The thing you want is a car. How can magic give you a car?

Well, directly, it can't. You can't do a spell to get a car, go to sleep that night, and then wake up the next morning expecting to find a brand new car in your driveway. That would be impossible, because it deals with the concept of "creating something out of nothing" and that magic simply doesn't exist.

But indirectly, magic can affect the world around you so as to bring a car into your sphere of existence so that you, ultimately, end up with a new car.

For instance, you cast a spell in which the desired result is to get a new car. You might do this with candle magic or call upon the Goddess for assistance. Maybe you'll use word magic or gems. Regardless of your decisions regarding the *type* of magic (we'll go over this later on in chapter six), your goal is the same: A new car.

So you cast your spell. It may take a couple of days to come about, or it could take longer. It could take weeks or even months. A lot of this is dependent on the spell, the complexity of the desired goal, and your personal intentions behind it.

But let's say in this case, it takes a couple of weeks. Over the course of those couple of weeks you a) receive a bonus at your work, b) have several friends who owe you money finally pay you back, and c) find the *exact car you were looking for* go on sale for half-price due to a blow-out, everything must go sale. Thanks to your bonus and your friends, you now have enough money to purchase your dream car at the sale price.

On the surface, all of these things not only look mundane, but coincidental. Would these things have happened without magic? Maybe, but maybe not. After all, your friends have owed you money for a long time – why choose now to pay you back? You've *never* gotten a bonus from work, what changed your boss's mind? And a half-priced, brand new car? Ridiculous!

That's how a spell works. It takes the realm of possibility and opens the channels so that the unlikely or the slow moving are redirected to come together at the exact right time to make your desires and goals come true. Magic is merely a force willing the world around us to bend and shift so that we might come to the things we seek.

But keep in mind one very important thing: You cannot create something that does not already exist.

Magic uses what is already in existence to bring us what we want, but if that want isn't already out there in some shape or form, then magic cannot bring that to us. You can't ask for a pet unicorn if there is no unicorn, but you might find yourself with a horse or a stuffed unicorn. This is why it's so important to know what you want and in what form you want it. We'll cover this later in chapter four.

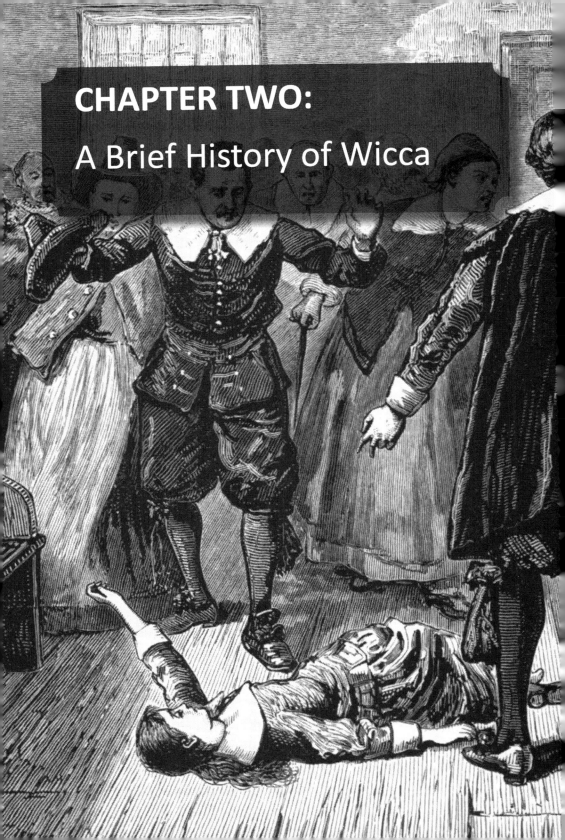

# CHAPTER TWO:
## A Brief History of Wicca

## CHAPTER TWO: A Brief History of Wicca

CREATION OF WICCA

### *The Persecution of Witches*

The term Wicca came from the old Latin term *wicce* meaning "wise one". It's pronunciation was closer to "witch-a" than to the hard "k" sound of Wicca, but the connotation is clear. To practice Wicca is to follow the path of wisdom and wherever that might lead you.

As I mentioned in chapter one, not every witch is a Wiccan. Wicca is a religion, while witch is a universal term for one who uses magic. This means that a witch could be good or bad, while a Wiccan, if practicing as the religion lays out, is going to be predominantly good, or at the very least neutral.

### Here's why that's important:

Witches have been persecuted for a very long time. From the onset of Christianity, witches – also known as pagans – have been accused of the witchcraft from the Bible. That means "devil worship". It's a Christian concept to explain things that one religion didn't understand of another. When Rome was conquering the world, much of the "old ways" were preserved, to an extent, so long as the people in question offered their fealty to the new empire. However, many from the British Isles refused to give in and fought for their right to be independent.

In more modern times, there were anti-witchcraft laws as late as 1951 in Britain, making the persecution of any traditions that might have been construed as "witchcraft" or witchcraft related very viable. Once the last of these laws were repealed, Wicca was made more publicly available through books written on the subject. Thus, it's possible that the religion itself actually existed before the publication of these books and was merely kept secret as a means of protecting those practicing.

In the United States, religious freedom was still an important part of the constitution and thus allowed for the practice of alternative religions, however, that would assume that "witchcraft" constituted an actual religion as opposed to merely the practice of magic. Most Christians were – and often still are – unwilling to accept this view and will condemn those who call themselves Wiccan simply for their differing beliefs and misconceptions on the part of those outside the religion.

Wicca as per its original conception was not these "old ways" but a new age conglomeration of past traditions that were reworked into a new, modern tradition that could apply to the people of today. Thus, when people say it is an *ancient* religion, they aren't necessarily wrong. But it's important to understand that while many of the traditions are taken from the old Celtic traditions, Wicca is a much more modern entity that was mainly conceived in the 1930s and revived in the fifties after the publication of several modern day "witchcraft" books that revealed many of the previously tightly held secrets of the religion.

Remember, Wicca may be considered relatively new, but the traditions upon which it's founded are ancient and predate even Christianity.

The Salem Witch Trials in the 1600s have been explained by hysteria brought about by strict religious views, economic tensions, and the threat of conflict with the Native Americans nearby as colonists spread farther and farther into their lands. It's also been explained by scholars as being brought about by actual witches – but not as Christians define them. Instead, that the people of Salem were persecuted for practicing an older religion that was steeped in mystery and magic. A practice that Christians didn't understand so thusly labeled as "witchcraft" which to them equated

SPIRIT

WATER

FIRE

## CHAPTER THREE: Basic Wiccan Beliefs

**THEOLOGY**

As I mentioned, Wicca is a nature based religion that allows for people from all walks of life without discrimination. The religion is all about finding a balance with the elements that make up the universe, including humanity itself. There are two main principles accepted by most, if not all, witches.

**The first is the Wiccan Rede**: "And ye harm none, do what ye will." This means simply that magic is limitless. You may do as you please with it, but do not use it for destructive reasons.

**The second is the Law of Three**: "What ye send out, return to thee, times three." This goes with the second, acting as both warning and promise. Send out only good things into the world as when they return to you – as they inevitably will – they were be three times as powerful as when you threw them out into the universe. If they are all positive things, then you will invite only positive things into your life.

### *The Elements*

There are five basic elements of the Craft. Earth, Air, Fire, Water, and what is known as Spirit. All but Spirit have some type of physical or visible manifestations (even air; you can *see* a tornado). This is because Spirit acts as the ether that ties everything together.

**Spirit is like magic.** It isn't so much a *thing* physically as it is a *will*. It is the force behind things, the ether that brings and ties us to one another. It has no physical form and is instead what we need it to be. It is malleable and as strong as we let it be. It's color is often associated with either white or purple (usually a lighter, lavender type color). Ultimately, it is whatever you visualize it as.

**Earth is the ground upon which we walk.** It is the embodiment of nature and when most of us consider the natural world, we think of the Earth elemental. Trees, rocks, dirt and moss. The forest, the jungle, the mountain, even the desert. These are all manifestations of the Earth elemental. Earth means stability. Calling upon Earth is asking for consistency, grounding, and even stubbornness. The Earth is reasonable, but remember that Earth is often associated with Mother Nature. This is because she can be cruel, but fair. It's associated color is green.

**Air is the wind.** It is the sky and the very air that we breathe. It is wily and finicky. It is playful, picking at your clothes and pulling at your hair, encouraging you to dance. Air is difficult to capture, impossible to keep, and yet it surrounds us everywhere. We are never truly alone when Air is there with us. To call for Air would be to call for fun and playfulness, to invite laughter into your life. But remember that Air is also inconsistent. It shifts as the wind shifts and that can make it seem flakey. It's associated color is usually yellow or gold. Sometimes it can be represented as a light blue, however this can conflict with Water and is thus usually given some incarnation of yellow.

**Fire is the heart of the earth**. If Air is the sky and Earth is the ground, the Fire is the molten rock beneath the surface. It is the lifeblood of the world, pumping passion and fire into everything it touches. It's the fire where you roast your marshmallows and the wildfire tearing through the nearby forest. That's important to remember about Fire: It gives life and passion to everything it touches, but it can also be a powerful, destructive force that waits and stops for no one. When you call on Fire, you had best be prepared for the intensity of the consequences. It's associated color is usually red, either bright or dark. Sometimes it may be displayed as orange.

**Water is the youth and sustenance of the earth.** Without water, nothing would survive. We, ourselves, are made up of mostly water and the earth is covered by seventy-five percent of it. Water is vitality and a natural, deep peace. Water is emotion and calm, the softness to the Earth's hardness, and a calm to the Fire's ferocity. To call on Water is to call on your own heart, the empathetic and compassionate side, but remember that Water isn't reasonable. It knows only what it feels and flows in that direction accordingly. It's associated color is almost always blue, dark or light. If it's represented by physical water, it may be considered "clear", but otherwise is shown as blue.

There are often masculinities and femininities associated with each of the Elementals, but they are ultimately facets of the Goddess (which is made up of both the Goddess *and* the God) and are thus genderless. If you must have them, first decide upon your own personal feelings on the matter. How do *you* view them? From there, you may find the actual genders often associated with each element.

**The Goddess and God**

Often considered a very "female friendly" religion, Wicca has two main deities. The Goddess and her consort, the God. It's important to understand that the Goddess and the God are actually *the same thing*. They are two sides of the same coin, different facets of the same diamond. They are a part of each other, even as they represent different aspects of the universe.

A quick note here. If you are following what is known as an "eclectic" path, you might have more deities than this – or you might have only the Goddess. These are valid beliefs, of course, but they stray from the typical definition of what a Wiccan specifically believes. While Wicca borrows largely from older Celtic traditions, it narrows down their monotheistic beliefs to simply two main entities: The Goddess and the God.

**The Goddess is the primary deity of the religion.** She is the driving power behind Wicca. The Goddess has three phases of existence. She is the Maiden, Mother, and Crone, each one representing a different stage of the natural cycle of the world. Each incarnation has a separate association and would be called upon for different reasons during a spell or ritual.

**The Maiden is innocence and purity**. She is youthful and vibrant, but naïve. The Mother is nurturing and sympathetic, but strong against external forces which might oppose her. And the Crone is wise. She is all-knowing and understanding, letting experience be her guide. She is reasonable, but forgiving.

**The God is the Goddesses consort**. Often represented as a horned god, he rises in power as the Goddess descends more into the harshness of winter. While the Goddess never relinquishes control entirely, she allows the hunter – the God – to reign in the barren months where her fruits – nature – are waning or slumbering. This is because the Goddess is the Crone in these months and is content to let wisdom guide the virility of the God, her lover. When spring returns, the Goddess becomes the Maiden and the God pursues her as a child might chase first love. When he catches her, it is towards the end of spring, summer on its heels and she is with child. This is where she becomes the Mother and takes power over her children again (the ecosystem, including humans). As summer wanes, so does her hold on the world, slowly allowing the God to return in force.

## Misconceptions

If you ask someone what a "Wiccan" is, they'll likely tell you something along the lines of "devil worshipper, witch, or hippie". This is because a lot of today's religions have overlapping concepts that get mixed up by those unaware of the practices.

For instance, the pentagram is a symbol often used in both Wiccan traditions and in witchcraft. It might also show up in Satanism and other devil-worshipping religions, but this is usually as an inverted pentagram (where the two points or "legs" of the star are pointed towards the top instead of the bottom, perhaps even creating an image of a goat or other horned creature). The inverted pentagram might be still used in witchcraft, but represents chaos instead of the devil. Because of this "chaotic" nature, the inverted pentagram is generally not used in Wiccan practices.

In addition to the misinformation out there about the symbols used in Wicca, there's a lot of misrepresentation found in the media today. From Charmed to The Secret Circle, it's easy to see where traditional practice of the Craft gets lost in translation. Suddenly we associate Wicca with people who control the elements (as physical manifestations) or think that demons — again, a Christian concept — are part of the Wiccan religion. This is made even more complicated when these fictional adaptations take actual pieces of the religion to give their fictional worlds a more "realistic" feel.

## CHAPTER FOUR: How to Practice

RITUAL ASPECTS OF THE CRAFT

### Casting a Circle

Later on I'll discuss altars and their purposes in the Craft, but first I feel it's important to talk about the basics of the magical aspect of Wicca. The most basic part of any spell or ritual is the circle. At first glance, it seems irrelevant or unimportant – after all, it's just a circle, right? But it's arguably the *most* important part of magical workings. Here's why.

Every spell deals with energy, as do rituals. I mentioned that magic is energy, a will that goes out into the world that is dictated by intent in order to mold the universe to suit our needs. Well, if magic is basically intention, then isn't there magic floating around out there coming from every person on the planet who is thinking and focusing on their own, personal intentions? The short answer is *yes*. And it's especially true because most people don't fully understand that they are doing this. To them, they are merely repeating a positive mantra before a presentation in the hopes that it goes well. Or they're focusing on picking the right outfit for a big date or meeting. These are mundane, everyday things that aren't magical in nature – but they

# CHAPTER FOUR :
## How to practice ritual aspects of the craft

## CHAPTER THREE: Basic Wiccan Beliefs

We see this in the use of a Book of Shadows, in the casting of circles, or the use of herbs and crystals to cast spells. Ultimately, these representations cause confusion and can give newcomers to the religion unrealistic expectations of what they will find here.

My advice as a cure for this is *do your research*. Figure out the truths of the Craft instead of taking it from Hollywood. That way you're less likely to be disappointed with what you find. Instead, you might find a true spiritual connection.

are a type of magic. Each one of these acts as a mini spell sent out into the world with little focus past the initial intent.

Which isn't necessarily bad or dangerous, but it can be problematic for those who are deliberately practicing magic. These energies might interfere with our own intentions, causing the spell to be less effective or go awry. If I'm trying to do a spell to banish something from my life and my neighbor is wishing for something to come *into* her life, then her intentions might clash with mine to either bring me the wrong thing or cancel out my own intentions.

The means of dealing with this confusion is very simple: **Cast a circle.**

Imagine a circle like a wall. Maybe like the wall to a well that goes down deep and sets up above ground, too. It's circular and made of stone and if you're in the well, no one's getting to you from the sides, right? A circle is similar in that way. It's a means of putting up walls – metaphorically as opposed to physically – that keep *your* energies in and *everyone else's* energies out. This allows your spell to be focused and more potent.

To cast a circle, you don't need anything,

## CHAPTER FOUR: How to Practice

although if you'd like to use something physical to draw the circle there are a couple of options. But first, you can cast a circle with nothing but your own mind. All you have to do is find north (always start your circle at north). Face north and imagine a beam of light forming on the ground in front of you. This beam shoots up from the ground in a golden light and as you move, it will follow you. Begin to turn in a clockwise motion, moving towards the east, south, west, and finally back to north. All along, imagine this light following your movements. This light will form your circle and it will act as a barrier between you and the outside world – so make sure you have everything you need for your magic working before you form your circle.

If you want to draw a physical circle, you have options also. You can use an athame (mentioned in the next chapter; similar to a dagger, but without the sharpness) to physically draw the circle in the ground. You can draw the circle using chalk, which is excellent for a wooden or concrete floor. Or you can use salt. Pour the salt liberally following the same idea as drawing the circle with light. Pour the salt around you, starting in the north and moving in a clockwise fashion.

As long as you and your spell items are within this circle, you are protected from those floating outside energies. When you finish with your spell, remember to close your circle. This means un-drawing your circle or erasing what you have physically drawn there. Some encourage the use of Widdershins (counterclockwise) to undo your circle, while others insist that you should undo it the same way you created it, moving clockwise. I encourage you to do what you feel most comfortable. Most magic is about doing what you feel is right.

**Spellcraft**

When I say "spellcraft" I'm referring to the working of magic using a spell, but it can also mean the creation of a spell, potion, or ritual. This is determined by context.

First, I'll go over the basics of how to create a spell. It can be very simple, or it can be complex. Like all magic it's determined by you. Before we begin, let me answer the question I know you're going to ask: *Does my spell have to rhyme?* Well, no, it doesn't. A spell can be a single word or a long poem or just a sentence or two. It just depends on you and what you need. That being said, I do recommend that you make your spell rhyme if it has multiple words in it. This is simply because *rhymes are easier to remember.* This means you'll spend less time focusing on how to get the words out or trying to remember them exactly and you can offer more energy to the spell itself.

So, creating a spell. You need three things to make a successful spell: Intention, specificity, and a little creativity. (You may want additional things like candles, herbs, or potions, but these three things above are all you *need* for a spell.)

## CHAPTER FOUR: How to Practice

Intention is the equivalent of purpose. What is the purpose of your spell? Say you want to do a prosperity spell. That's perfect for intention. It tells you what you're trying to accomplish and gives you a good idea of what you'll need for the spell (if you want to include herbs or other things). But it's not very specific. And that's where our second thing comes in.

**Specificity.** Your intent is sort of vague. It's a concept, what you want from your spell, but specificity is all about *what you intend to get from your spell.* For example, what I deem as prosperous might be different than what you deem as prosperous. Maybe I think of owning a successful ranch as being prosperous, while you imagine living in a high rise apartment. These differences will directly influence your spell and can make your spell either weak, ineffective, or simply lacking in the necessary potency. So it's important to be specific when you write your spell. (This is why one-word spells should only be used for very general concepts, like health, good fortune, or sending good energy somewhere.) Specificity comes in the form of wording mostly. An example (continuing with our prosperity purpose): If you want prosperity to come to you in the form of being a successful career wo/man, then say specifically, "make my career prosperous, my endeavors successful" or something to that effect. It's important here to include something specific about *your* goals.

**Creativity**. This part comes down to you and it changes your spell's complexity. Do you want to burn incense, call on the Mother Goddess, light a candle for each of the four elementals, and cast your circle in the light of the full moon on midnight? You can certainly do that! Or you can leave this very basic and say that you're casting your circle in your own home, saying a quick spell, and thanking the energies of the universe for helping you out. The creativity is in the ritual and that comes down to what your personal preferences are. For a simple spell, worry only about getting your intentions right and being specific. Then get to the more creative stuff like rhyming, burning candles, and summoning deities to your aide.

## CHAPTER FOUR: How to Practice

**Now that you've got the basics of creating a spell down, I'll move on to how to use a spell. A lot of this goes along with the creation of the spell – intention and specificity – but to actually use the spell there are a couple of important rules.**

1. Always cast a circle. It doesn't matter what you're doing, casting a circle is important because it keeps your energies separate from those around you. It makes your spell more potent.

2. Cleanse your circle of negativity.

3. Cast your spell within the circle.

4. Thank whichever deities or elements or powers you might have asked for aide in your spell. At the very least, thank the universe for listening.

5. Close your circle. Always.

## CHAPTER FOUR: How to Practice

6. Ground yourself by sending the leftover energies of your spell back into the earth so that they can be reabsorbed and aren't left floating around – or worse, clogging up your body with unused potential! (You can ground by putting your bare hands or feet on the ground, or a nearby tree – something solid and natural – and imagining those magical forces leaving through your body and out your toes and fingertips. When you're done, you'll feel a little lighter and a lot calmer.)

**You can add more ritual if you'd like, but always remember these six steps when you cast your spell. Without them, there's no telling where your magic will go, what it'll do, and what's interfering with it.**

# CHAPTER FIVE:
## Tools and Altars, THE TOOLS OF WORSHIP

# CHAPTER FIVE: Tools and Altars

THE TOOLS OF WORSHIP

**What is an Altar and Do I Need One?**

It's important to know that most witches have an altar – and no, technically, you don't need one. When you're starting out as a witch, an altar might be a little too expensive to invest in. Ideally, the religious necessities of the Craft would be free, but in today's capitalist society, it's not likely. So until you know if Wicca is right for you, there are some ways around the need for a "permanent" altar. But first, what is an altar?

An altar is simply a place for you to worship. It's like a church or a temple, but more personal and on a smaller scale. If you are a member of a coven, you might have a coven altar, but even then you will likely have a personal one there in your own home. An altar might also be used to cast spells, depending on the spell and the witch. Just remember that if you are casting at your altar, you still must draw your circle around your entire space, yourself inside it.

Generally speaking, an altar is a raised platform or dais. It can also be simply a cloth laid out on the floor that is used *only* for the purpose of serving as your altar. Usually you want something more permanent – a small table or desk or perhaps just a solid wooden box that is slightly raised from the floor – but in a pinch, you can use a cloth instead. If you have the ability and space, you might try to put your altar outside. (This is ideal because it's out in nature, however, it can be problematic if you live in a place with a lot of rain or a lot of sunlight, as these things can melt or ruin what's left on your altar. If you do have an outside altar, maybe using a stump or block of wood, then I recommend either setting things up each time or having some sort of protective covering for it.)

There are different items a witch might have on their altar, as each altar is specific to the witch. It's very personalized, so do what feels right to you. That being said, there are a handful of items every witch will have on her altar.

**An athame**. At first glance, this will be a "knife", but it's important to understand that this object might be shaped similarly to a knife, it is never used for cutting. The tip acts more like a wand might, a director of energy. To use it for the destructive purpose of cutting, even in ritual, would contaminate the energies of the athame. Thus, it's alright if your athame is blunt, similar to a letter opener.

**A small hand bell**. Typically silver, though you can certainly get one more suited to your tastes, the ringing of the bell is used to clear energies in the air. These might be negative energies or merely those that have been left over from previous spellworkings. By clearing these energies, you've opened your circle up to the energies you need for your specific spell. It also allows for a clear and clean space for speaking to the Goddess, which is the main purpose of your altar.

**At least four candles.** These candles are color coordinated to match the elementals mentioned in chapter three. They are often referred to "directional" candles instead of elemental candles, because they represent the four corners or the for directions – north, south, east, and west. A red candle represents Fire and the South. A blue candle represents Water and the West. A green candle represents Earth and the North. And finally a yellow candle represents Air and the East. These candles should be placed in the correct positions according to these directions (so your green candle should always be set in the northern direction). You may have an additional white candle in the center of your altar to represent the Goddess and Spirit. This is optional and dependent on your personal preference as there are other objects that directly represent the Goddess. Additionally, you might add in other candles specific to spellwork. I'll talk more on that in a moment.

**You should have a cup or chalice.** The chalice represents the Goddess specifically, it's shape and design resembling in some ways the natural curves of a woman. The cup is important because it holds water, which is often represented as the Goddess in ritual.

**Thus, water is another must have on every altar**. It should be contained in either the chalice or in a bowl also on your altar. You can mix the water with salt – which represents the God and is also an important thing to have on your altar – or have the water and salt separate (in such a case, you would have the water in the cup and the salt on either a plate or a bowl).

**You'll have a separate, empty dish**. It's usually a type of curved plate, caught between a plate and a bowl. This is your offering dish and will hold whatever you offer up in your prayers to the Goddess. It can be flowers, food, or other objects (crystals, feathers, dolls, etc.).

**Finally, you'll want a pentacle**. This is representative of the five elements, all connected and contained within a witch's circle and is thus one of the most important symbols in the Craft. The pentacle can be drawn directly on your altar, it can be on an altar cloth – which would cover your altar platform – or it can be on a plate or other object. Just so long as it is on the altar, a reminder of that which we are all connected to.

These are the main objects that every witch will have on her altar. You may include others as you see fit and it's encouraged to have physical representations for each of the elements also, but if need be, candles are enough.

## Additional Tools

There are other tools that you might be interested in having on your altar. I've listed them below and what their purposes or meanings are.

**Wand**. Similar to an athame, the wand is a means of directing energies. Some might prefer this to an athame, as it's typically wood and occasionally topped with a crystal of some type. I recommend against replacing the athame, however, as the flat surface of the athame can be useful in moving elements in your altar (such as adding the salt to the water).

**Feather.** A feather is usually used to represent the Air elemental for those who wish for physical representations on their altars. As feathers move air efficiently, they might also be used to cleanse the air of negativity.

**Crystal**. A crystal is usually used for healing, especially a clear crystal like Quartz. They channel energies and can be placed on the body or held in your hands to draw those energies out or to concentrate them, depending on your intentions. As they're drawers of energy, they can be used on your altar, but make sure you know what kind of crystal you have.

**Stone**. A stone, usually a dark, opaque color, can be used for grounding energies that you have collected. Instead of banishing them or clearing them from a circle, stones send these energies back into the earth so that they aren't left to wander or interfere with other spellworking.

**Bundle of Sage**. Like incense, you light the tip of the sage bundle and use the smoke to purify the air. It's similar to the bell in that it clears away negative energies, but unlike the bell, it does not remove those energies that might still linger from previous spells. So keep that in mind when using Sage. It is a means of purifying a space and banishing negativity, so it's harmless to use, and even encouraged for use in your home, especially if you've just moved to a new house.

# CHAPTER SIX:
## Types of Magic

## CHAPTER SIX: Types of Magic

**MAGIC**

*Herbal Magic*

At first, everyone thinks that a witch's kitchen is full of ridiculous thing like bat's wing and dragon's blood (which most witches do have as incense, but that's another story). But really, most people have magical ingredients in their kitchen. They just don't know it. Here's a quick breakdown of some of the most common spices in your kitchen and the things they might be used for. I've listed them as either "edible" or "non-edible" so you know which ones are safe to consume and which are for ritual only.

**Allspice** *(Edible)*:

- Money
- Luck
- Health
- 

**Basil** *(Edible)*:

- Brings love
- Wealth
- Sympathy
- Dispels fear and other weaknesses

## CHAPTER SIX: Types of Magic

**Bay leaves** *(Edible)*:

- To build psychic powers
- Strength
- Wealth
- Helpful for building success

**Caraway** *(Edible)*:

- Protection from theft and negativity
- A means of building trust

**Cinnamon** *(Edible)*:

- Spirituality
- Success
- Prosperity
- Strength
- Power

**Clove** *(Edible)*:

- Youthful love
- Protection
- To give someone the ability to see past a façade

## CHAPTER SIX: Types of Magic

**Coriander** *(Edible)*:

- Love
- Well-being
- Intelligence

**Cumin** *(Edible)*:

- Fidelity
- Protection
- To protect against theft
- To exorcise unhealthy or dangerous energies

**Dill** *(Edible)*:

- Protection
- Money
- Lust

**Flour** *(Edible)*:

- Revealing the hidden truth
- Consistency

**Garlic** *(Edible)*:

- Hex breaking
- Banishing negativity
- Protection

## CHAPTER SIX: Types of Magic

**Ginger** *(Edible)*:

- Health
- Cleansing
- Vitality

**Mustard** *(Edible)*:

- Faith
- Mental alertness

**Nutmeg** *(Edible)*:

- Prosperity
- Luck
- Breaking of a hex
- Useful for removing or thwarting curses.

**Parsley** *(Edible)*:

- Luck
- Protection from accidents

**Pepper** *(Edible)*:

- Cleansing
- Purification
- Protection
- Banishing

**Red Pepper** *(Edible)*:

- Energy
- Vitality
- Strength

**Peppermint** *(Edible)*:

- Helpful for purification
- Sleep
- Prophetic dreams
- Useful in psychic workings.

**Sage** *(Edible)*:

- To purify a place
- To bring about wisdom
- To help with grief and loss
- Promotes health and longevity

**Salt** *(Edible)*:

- Cleansing
- Purification
- Grounding

**Vanilla** *(Edible)*:

- Love
- Lust
- Passion
- Useful in love or sex magic.

And here are a few more that are easy to find, but maybe you don't have hanging around in your spice rack.

**Hazelnut** *(Edible)*:

- Wisdom
- Fertility

**Lavender** *(Edible)*:

- Spiritual vision
- Acknowledgement of self
- Comfort

**Lilac** *(Edible – blossoms)*:

- Love
- Youth
- Joy
- Fastidiousness

## CHAPTER SIX: Types of Magic

**Rose** *(Edible)*:

- Love
- Faithfulness
- Friendship

**Saffron** *(Edible)*:

- Bounty
- Leadership
- Prosperity

**Valerian** *(Edible – seeds and leaves)*:

- Dreams
- Astral projection
- Love
- Brings about harmony and reconcile
- Useful for sleep

## CHAPTER SIX: Types of Magic

**Wow! That's a great list, right? And now you're wondering:** *how do I use them?*

It's pretty simple actually, so don't worry. You don't need to have a little garden, plant them at midnight, and harvest them only in the light of the full moon. (Yes, there are some spells that suggest you do these things as they'll make your spell more powerful, but they aren't necessary so long as you pick the right plant for the right spell.) Instead, just using the dried herbs you have in your kitchen will do in a pinch – though if you have the space and the opportunity, having a personal garden will save you some serious cash and give your spells a more personal touch.

In chapter four, I talked about spellcrafting. About how your intentions were important for the spell, but so were your words. Here, the same thing is true. Your intentions and the intentions of your spell are very important for the overall success of your spell, but so are the herbs you use. There are some spells and rituals that call for the use of certain herbs and in these cases, they will tell you how they should be used.

For instance, before starting your spell, you cast your circle. That circle can be drawn in chalk or even just visualized as a ring of pure white light. But an alternative is to create a circle out of salt. Because salt is a cleanser, purifier, and a grounder, it serves multiple purposes. It consecrates your space and adds extra purification to your spell. At the same time, it also grounds your magic, which is important, because excess magic can leak out into the world if it's not properly dealt with.

But spells aren't the only thing you might use herbs for – or even the primary one. While spells are primarily focused on the written word and ritual, there are other types of magic which are effective all the same, but are more of inactive spells. They are charms and satchels, passive spells that work in the background. They are wards against evil or bringers of luck. Here are some ideas for using herbs in your magical workings.

## Satchels

A satchel is basically a collection of objects or herbs that are gathered together with a specific purpose in mind. These are largely comprised of herbs, though they might also contain things like stones or gems, small twigs, sacred items or metals, and even papers with written words on them. What goes inside the satchel is up to you and should depend on what your intentions are. Here's an example:

### For Protection

- White or woven bag, small
- Pepper
- Parsley
- Garlic
- Dill

## CHAPTER SIX: Types of Magic

- Clove
- Caraway
- Allspice
- Coriander
- Salt

These herbs all, in some way or another, represent or help with protection of either a specific nature or very generally. But if you notice, I also included salt for purification and coriander for well-being. This is because, while protection is our goal, it's never a bad idea to include some sort of cleanser or purifier to encourage protection in the most well-meaning of sense. And it's also not a bad idea to include an herb that's more specific and encourages the well-being of an individual. This is because protection could come in many forms. You could protect your house – but that doesn't necessarily protect you if you're not in it. Or it could protect you from dying, but not being seriously injured. By adding in coriander, you are telling your satchel that you are aiming for the "well-being" of someone, not just their ultimate survival. So don't be afraid to add in additional herbs that maybe aren't specific to your spell, but might give additional distinctness to it. Just make sure that you think through what they might be telling the universe you're asking for.

Additionally, if you wanted to, you could add

in other things. You might add in a note that asks for "safety" or a crystal to direct energy or cleanse the negativity in the area. Or maybe you add a dollop of dried green wax to tie this spell to Earth and ground it in practicality. This is up to you. Think of what you want and what you need, then draw up a bag accordingly.

## *Cooking*

The easiest way to use herbs is actually something you probably do every day: Cooking. As I mentioned, you'll find most of these spices in your kitchen right now without having to go out and buy anything. That means you *already use them* on an at least semi-regular basis. This means that these helpful properties are already in your system, but they aren't as powerful as they are because you haven't had the knowledge of their purpose. I said earlier that *intention* is the fuel for magic and how can you have focused intention without the knowledge of what you are using?

But now that you know what you're using, you can harness those properties to create a meal that is not just delicious, but magically potent. If you want some excellent recipes, I recommend *The Kitchen Witch* by Patricia Telesco. She offers a large list of herbs and their uses as well as provides a whole cookbook full of wonderful recipes appropriate for the witch and the average person alike.

Recipes aside, the basics of herbal magic through cooking are very similar to creating a satchel, but it's a little more complicated than that. It's because now you're not just throwing things together by magical property, but also by their taste and how they work with each other. You probably don't want to put cinnamon and mustard together. Thankfully, most of the herbs listed above don't directly cause problems if used together, but it can get tricky to get the portions right in combination with one another. If you throw things together, focusing only on their magical properties, you're at a higher risk of ending up with one big failure of a meal.

A way around that is to separate your magical intentions by dish. Want to encourage travel in your life? Make cornbread. Want more energy in your life? Make a spicy red pepper chicken dish. Want to add more passion in your life? Add a vanilla desert. By making a meal with several dishes, you decrease the chances of adding conflicting herbs, while still reaching your desired results. So look through your everyday recipes and determine their strongest magical properties. From there, add some thought and intention while you're making them to create a powerful and tasty meal. For deliberately magical recipes, consider concocting your own or looking for a witch-specific cookbook (like the one mentioned above.

## Potions

Potions are the middle ground between cooking and satchels. Although you can certainly make them edible, they are more often meant to act like charms or to be used as skin creams and lotions, perfumes, or ceremonial tinctures. With that in mind, while these may be edible (but may not be, so be sure to check first), they are not made with taste in mind as they would be in cooking.

Potions involve adding herbs – fresh if possible – to a small pot (or cauldron) filled with water or wine. (Wine is often used for ceremonial purposes, but if you're adding heat, I recommend water rather than wine, especially if you plan to consume this.) While stirring in a clockwise manner with a wooden spoon, add in your herbs as you focus on your intention for the spell. Allow them to boil down some and when they've become pulpy for fresh herbs or smoothed out for dried or powdered herbs, take them off the heat. Allow this to cool, then add to vials or another container with a water tight lid. Some potions are encouraged to steep for several days, while others are meant to be left alone, a type of charm or ward on the house. If you intend to consume your potions, refrigerate until use.

Please note that if you are planning on drinking or otherwise consuming your potions, be sure to check that all of your ingredients are edible as potions can make you ill if there are any poisonous plants included in them.

## Candle Magic

Candles are a staple in any witch's magical arsenal. They have an energy all their own as they burn, transforming from one thing to another while they melt, from liquid to solid. This transformation carries power and is extremely helpful in magical workings. This is especially true for those wanting a physical representation of their working magic. A candle allows for the witch to focus on something *real*, here in the physical world, which can be especially useful when beginning your journey into magic.

There are several things that are important to remember when working with candles. First, you should be considering their color when working them into a spell. Colors have magical significance and connotations. It's important to pick the right ones to make sure you're performing the spell as accurately as possible. Second, whenever you're using fire for any sort of spell or ritual, it's important to be prepared. Keep things away that might catch fire and always have water handy to put things out. Third, candle magic is as simple or as complex as you'd like to make it. You can include carved symbols into the wax, add oils or herbs to be burned with the candle, or use candles that are deliberately shaped like specific things – such as the Goddess.

## *Color connotations.*

- **Red**. Passion and strength. This can be used for power spells or for love spells, but remember its potency.

- **Pink.** Love and kindness. This can also be used for love spells, but with a more innocent or friend-specific tone to them. This will have a much sweeter result.

- **Orange.** Courage and enthusiasm. Used for spells asking for bravery or resolve. Can also be used to add additional oomph to other spells.

- **Yellow.** Optimism 1and creativity. Used for spells regarding muses or other forms of creative inspiration.

- **Green.** Stability and abundance.

## CHAPTER SIX: Types of Magic

Used for money spells, gain, or if you want to add resolution to your spells.

- **Blue.** Emotion, tranquility, and patience. Used for meditation or spells invoking calm emotions such as a deep, nurturing love.

- **Purple.** Spirituality and enlightenment. Used for spells asking for guidance, dream magic, or astral projection.

- **Black.** Banishing negativity, release, and wisdom or mystery. Used for banishing spells or spells to ward something off. To undo another's negative magic upon you.

- **white.** Purity cleansing, peace, and balance. A white candle can stand in for any of the others, so long as you determine its purpose before you begin your spell. It is representative of the Goddess oftentimes and acts as an easy representation of just about anything.

## Using candles is a four step process

(not including the casting of your circle and other prayers or rituals you might include)

**One:** Prepare your candle. Fill it with whatever intent you have for your magic. Carve whatever symbols you might want. Anoint it with oils or herbs as you deem necessary.

**Two:** Light the candle.

**Three:** Focus on the candle's purpose and your intent. What is your purpose here? If you have any written words to go with this, you would read them here. Let the candle burn as long as you need to.

**Four:** Thank those energies you called upon for your magical workings, then blow out the candle. Make sure it has finished burning before putting up.

# CHAPTER SEVEN:
## Types of Practice

## CHAPTER SEVEN: Types of Practice

### Solitary versus Coven Practice

Although there are many different facets of the Craft – eclectic, pagan, Wiccan, etc. – There are ultimately only two ways to *practice*: Solitary or in a Coven. But what's the difference?

Very basically, the difference between being a solitary practitioner and being part of a coven is that solitary is just as it sounds: You practice by yourself. When you belong to a coven, your practice includes not just yourself but other witches who belong to the same coven.

Typically, a coven is a group of thirteen witches. This is the ideal number, but ultimately you only *need* a minimum of three witches to form a practicing coven. The number three represents the first "complete" number in that it has a beginning, middle, and end. Thus, three witches may create group magic successfully while two witches might feel incomplete. Thirteen has its own importance, largely based on the 13 moon calendar, in which there are thirteen moon cycles despite there being only twelve months. The phases are important in much of the magical workings in witchcraft and thus the number is significant to witches. (I'll talk about the esbats, which are lunar based, later on.) This is why it's ideal for witches to have thirteen members and will often strive to not go over this number.

That being said, with the growing popularity of witchcraft, covens may expand to include more than the standard thirteen.

A coven differs from solitary practice not just because there are other members included. Unlike solitary witches, in a coven there is a hierarchy in place. A coven will have a High Priestess or Priest who will lead the coven. They'll make decisions regarding ceremonies and rituals and will help with larger group magics. A solitary practitioner is led only by themselves and their personal connection to the Goddess. This isn't to say that a coven's High Priestess will have absolute control over its members, however. Instead, it means that with larger groups of people it becomes more important to have a leader to keep everyone on the same page with what's going on. This helps to avoid conflict and it keeps lines of power and communication open. This also helps to initiate new members and help them to learn the specific ways of that coven.

Covens will celebrate festivals together, do group magics, and help initiate new witches into the fold. They might oversee training in the Craft and sometimes offer titles to indicate what stage of growth the witch might be. These might be general and applicable to most practitioners of the Craft (like High Priestess which is a widely known term) or be specific to that coven. Each cove is different and will have their own guiding rules agreed upon by all members.

## CHAPTER SEVEN: Types of Practice

Although being a part of a coven is appealing to many witches – since there is no centralized church or similar structure, practicing can become a lonely religion – it is not always practical. For those who live in smaller communities that may not have a large population of witches in the area, or for people who don't have the time to commit regularly to ceremonies, it might be more beneficial to be a solitary practitioner. Ultimately, it's up to the individual to decide what's right for them and to take into account their specific situation.

# CHAPTER EIGHT :
## The Wiccan Festivals

**Samhain**
1 November

**Mabon**
21-24 September

**Lughnasadh**
1 August

**Yule**
23 December

**Imbolc**
2 February

**Ostara**
19-22 March

**Beltane**
1 May

**Midsummer**
19-23 June

# CHAPTER EIGHT: The Wiccan Festivals

**Sabbats**

A sabbat is a ritual celebration usually indicative of the season or of the Goddess and God specifically. There are eight in total, each marking a section of what is known as the Witch's Wheel. The Witch's Wheel is named so because it looks like a wheel, with each spoke marking one of the eight seasonal sabbats. It represents the changing of the seasons, but also the inevitability that they will return. It is birth, life, death, and rebirth all over again. Sometimes the Witch's Wheel might also be referred to as a Seasonal Wheel or Wheel of the Year.

**Samhain.** Samhain is arguably the most well-known of the witch's sabbats, though its celebration and tradition varies in the more secular communities. Celebrated on October 31st (or November 1st depending on your tradition), Samhain – pronounced sow-een – is also known as All Hallow's Eve or Halloween today. Some of the secular traditions of dressing up, passing out candy, or indulging in all that fun spookiness are actually ideas that have been borrowed from the practice of witches. Dressing up is to guard against spirits that have crossed over and might try and take you back with them. Passing out candy – or offering some other type of food – is a means of honoring the dead and giving them a gift on the one night of the year where they might come and visit us again. Finally, all of that spooky fun is because Halloween is the time of year where things cross over. Fall is heading out and winter is arriving, leaving us in a land of death and sleep. For the one night of Halloween, that line between life and death is blurred, opening up communication between those two realms.

Traditionally, the Samhain ritual will be celebrated at night, outdoors if possibly, and include fall symbols and foods – fall leaves and branches, reds, yellows, and oranges, squashes and pumpkins, harvested foods that might not preserve well during the winter months such as apples, certain grains or breads. Remember that it's extra important to include an offering during Samhain as you're not just providing sustenance for the Goddess and God, but also for the dead who have crossed over to visit you during this time. So make sure you have extra during your ritual for those attendees that you might not see in physical form.

## CHAPTER EIGHT: The Wiccan Festivals

If you would like to commune with the dead or do ritual magic involving divination, now would be the best time of the year to do so. Again, the line between worlds is thinnest during this time and thus allows for more open communication.

**Yule**. Celebrated on December 21st, this festival is connected closely to the Christian's Christmas. Instead of the birth of Jesus, this festival celebrates the death of the Goddess as she prepares to be reborn. Here she is the Crone, having left the Horned God to reign over the barren and cold lands until she is ready to once again be born as the Maiden in the spring. The God is at his height during the Yule festival, but the Goddess should not be forgotten for during this time she sacrifices her own self for the continuation of the Witch's Wheel.

**Imbolc** (or Candlemas). Celebrated on February 2nd, is a traditional ceremony which invites Spring back into our lives. If Yule is the tradition of the Crone Goddess passing from her hard life, then Imbolc is the celebration of her return. Here she comes back as the young Maiden, youthful and joyous, she brings with her a return of the vibrant colors and flowers of the world. Nature returns more boisterous than before. Here it's important to celebrate life and the return of another season. Celebrate with flowery dishes, light wines or grape juices, and light foods instead of some of the heavier dishes you might have during winter.

**Ostara.** Observed on March 22$^{nd}$, this festival celebrates the Spring Equinox. If Imbolc celebrates the rebirth of the Goddess, then Ostara is her youth and life. Largely celebrated as a fertility festival, this is the time to celebrate love, joy, and the creation of life. You might offer up eggs, plant in your personal garden, or replace those things in your life that have gone stale with new, vital things that will bring you health and happiness. This might be as simple as the food in your fridge or as complex as the unwelcome people in your life. Again, focus on the lighter dishes here, though oftentimes this festival includes breads and grains as a large part of the celebration.

**Beltane.** Observed on May 1$^{st}$, this is the continuation of the spring rites. Beltane is the focus of love and romance – and again, fertility – where the Goddess and God have both matured into young adults and might make love again to conceive the world. Beltane is sacred in that it represents a time to protect that which has grown – animals, gardens, kids – and to celebrate the continuation of the coming harvest season. This is an excellent time to celebrate love and to bring up those around you with encouragement and patience. Meals should focus on milks, eggs, and grains. You may also include apples or certain types of berries.

**Litha** (or Midsummer). Celebrated on June 21$^{st}$, this festival follows the Summer Solstice. At this point in time, the Goddess has become the Mother. She has given birth to the world and now watches over it with her patience and goodness. This celebration is all about nurturing, patience, and being thankful for the blessings surrounding us. That being said, this is an unusual festival in that, while it is primarily focusing on the abundance of summer around us and the health of the world, there is also the undeniable sense of what is coming. The Mother Goddess has already begun her shift towards Crone and amidst all the goodness, there is a twinge of sadness. This is the peak of abundance and thus all that comes after must be less, in some fashion or another. This means that it is also a festival that marks preparation. The beginning of the end.

**Lughnasadh** (or Lammas). Observed on August 1st, Lughnasadh is the beginning of the three major harvest festivals (Lughnasadh, Mabon, and Samhain). Here people have begun to harvest grains after growing them all season and are beginning the preparations to keep them through the harder winter months. Lughnasadh is about grains, blessings, and preservation. But it is also about a fair trade. If you've struck a bargain, see it through. You might play games or sports as a means of settling disputes and you should be more focused on weather also. Pay attention to what the world is telling you. Breads and fruits will be the staple of this harvest, especially focusing on that which will not last through the winter.

**Mabon.** Celebrated September 21$^{st}$, this festival marks the Fall Equinox. Second of the harvest festivals, this one focuses more on corns, vegetables, and any fruits that might be picked later in the season. It's popular during this festival to make dolls out of corn husks or create talismans for good fortune and a good season. It's important here to be thankful, grateful, and to celebrate the waning warmer months while welcoming the inevitable winter. Again, your main staples should be fruits, but if you have baked goods, focus more on corn than grain.

### *Esbats*

There are four traditionally celebrated esbats and they are all directly related to the phases of the moon. Although these might be celebrated regularly just as sabbats, they are not as important of festivals. This isn't that they don't have their purpose or that they aren't a good idea to observe, but while sabbats are the crux of the Wiccan tradition, esbats are used more commonly during the practice of magic. Thus, if you're not planning on working magic for that particular esbat – they each occur at least once every month – then it isn't strictly necessary to ritually observe them. That being said, it's encouraged to pay attention to the moon and give her your attention when you can. After all, the moon is the Goddess's most sacred symbol.

***Full Moon.*** This is when the moon is at its largest and most complete.

***Waning Moon.*** To wane is to decrease in either size or vigor. In the case of the moon, this is the stage when the moon is transitioning from full to new. This would be a good time to work banishing magic, as it suggests a decrease in power. Thus, if you're removing negativity from your life, then doing so as the moon gets smaller would be beneficial to your spellcasting.

**New Moon.** Also known as a Dark or Black Moon, this is when it looks as though there is no moon in the sky at all.

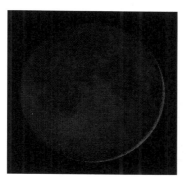

**Waxing Moon.** Opposite of the Waning Moon, this is when the moon is growing in size. It's transitioning between new and full. Because this is the stage of growing, it's a good time to cast spells regarding an increase in prosperity or success, or to bring something into your life. This is when the moon is gaining in power, which means that spells encouraging gain are perfect during this phase.

# CHAPTER NINE :
## Book of shadows

## CHAPTER NINE: Book of Shadows

### What is a Book of Shadows?

A Book of Shadows (sometimes also called a grimoire) is a mixture of a cookbook, a journal, and a history book. This is a deeply personal part of the Craft that is literally different for every witch. While some of these books might be passed down from generation to generation through a family or could be combined when working within a coven, it is generally accepted that you will have your own, personal Book of Shadows. This can be for a variety of reasons – maybe you're a solitary witch, maybe you're the first of your family, maybe you need a personal reference with you at all times. But ultimately, you should have your own book because it *is* so personal. What you put in will be indicative of your personal studies and experiences with the Craft, which may not match up with a separate person. And it's especially important if you're a solitary practitioner as you won't have others to share or reference with.

Although most people think of a Book of Shadows purely as a magical spellbook, it's important to understand that this is much more than that. It can, of course, include your personal spells, but it also lists magic ingredients, anecdotes, dedications to the Goddess and God. It may list personal experiences or a family tree showing your practicing ancestors. What's included is dependent on you and what you value, and that's why it's so important that you embark on your own journey to discover it.

Today, you can purchase very nice, fancy blank journals to act as your Book of Shadows. Many are even labeled as such and might be decorated with symbols of the Craft or various other embossing. And there is absolutely nothing wrong with using one of these premade books. However, if you have the means, I suggest making your own book. Create the paper, buy the leather (if you're going to use leather; you could also use cloth or something similar to cardboard or a thicker paper mix) and bind it all yourself. Yes, this is a lot more involved, but again I mention how deeply personal this book will be to you. It is yours and holds your life within it. So the book itself should be personal, too.

That being said, if you would rather, you can buy a book from your local bookstore or even create a digital Book of Shadows. I encourage you to handwrite your book, but it's up to you and if you feel more comfortable at your computer, then by all means do that. It's up to you. Do what feels right.

**What Should I Include in My Own Book of Shadows?**

Ultimately, a Book of Shadows can have whatever you want it to. It is your personal record, so you should include anything you find personally helpful. That being said, there are two things that every Book of Shadows should have: A list of herbs and their properties, and

## CHAPTER NINE: Book of Shadows

spells and rituals (ones that you yourself have tried and feel are successful; it does no good to include spells that don't work).

That being said, there isn't really any limit to what you can include in your personal book. Treat this like a journal of your experiences with the Craft. This means that as you learn new information, make notes of it in your book. If you find new herbs that you didn't know before, add them to your list. If you find a new bit of information about the Goddess or about sixteenth century Celtic practices, make a note of that, too. Whatever *you* think is important, you should include in this book. If you find that you have a specific ritual you really like for Samhain, then write it down and include it along with recipes, guides for candle-making, preferred soaps for purification. Anything. This book is a guide to how you practice. It will be unique entirely to you.

For those who might be interested in a more specific guide, I've included a few suggestions below. Take what you'd like and leave out all the rest.

- Personal dedication to the study of the Craft. (Just a personal statement saying when and why you've chosen to become Wiccan.)

- List of herbs and their magical properties.

- Spells, organized by type – Love, protection, purification, luck, etc.

- Satchel recipes.
- Potions.
- Magical crafts – such as corn husk dolls for Mabon.
- Rituals – including for the Sabbats and Esbats, but also in general.
- Information about the Goddess and the God.
- Personal experiences of magic in your life.
- Magical items – such as those on your altar.
- Any drawings or illustrations you might find pertinent to your Craft.

# CHAPTER TEN:
## Divination

## CHAPTER TEN: Divination

### Runes

Runes are an alphabet used to divine situations or even to predict the future. Generally, the runic alphabet are inscribed on stones or small pieces of wood, each one carrying only one runic symbol. Each rune has its own meaning, so the alphabet is not so much used to transcribe words as it is to mark events, things, or emotions depending on the reading.

There are twenty-four different runic symbols (or letters), each one with its own separate meaning. Additionally, there is a twenty-fifth rune that is simply blank. Reading runes can be difficult at first, because if you don't have them memorized you'll spend much of the reading deciphering the meanings in relation to each other and their individual location.

Casting runes is when you take your runic alphabet (stones or wood), and toss them onto a mat, a cloth, or within a drawn circle. The important thing about this is that you use a dedicated space for casting. This means that you wouldn't use this mat or cloth for anything but casting runes. Drawing a circle allows a little more leeway in that you can draw a new circle every time and do it just about anyway. So long as this is the only thing you use the circle for – and you draw it and erase it before and after every reading – then this is a perfectly acceptable place to cast your runes.

## Runes GUIDE

**Mannaz.** Meaning humanity on an individual level, skills and ability, having this in your circle means that you should embrace the physicality of your person as well as your personal skills. Accept the things that you are good at with grace and admit to the things that are beyond your reach.

**Gebo.** This rune means generosity and partnerships. It can be in regards to either business or personal relationships, and is generally a positive aspect. If it's found facedown, it might imply a relationship on the rocks, uncertainty, or one side of the relationship being closed off from the other.

## CHAPTER TEN: Divination

**Ansuz.** This is associated with communication and wisdom, scholarly and knowledge. This might be the written or spoken word. If this symbol is received within the circle, it might mean that communication is opening or that knowledge is going to become available. If facedown, this knowledge is obscured or deliberately hidden.

**Othila.** Meaning ancestral family and personal inheritance, this rune suggests that you need to embrace your lineage. It's important to know where you come from in order to understand where you are going.

**Uruz.** This rune is associated with power, strength, and action. This can mean bravery or force and if it shows up inside the circle, then you will likely encounter a burst of strength or energy in your life. If it shows up facedown, then you may be uncertain about something in your life or indecisive. Outside the circle may mean that a force is coming or influencing your life without your direct knowledge or say.

**Perth.** Associated with secrets, mystery, and destiny. If found within the circle, this might suggest that there are unknown factors influencing your life or that destiny is fast approaching. What is to come may be unknowable until its arrival and it may thus also be unavoidable. Should you find this facedown, it could represent a secret awaiting revelation or something that is simply impossible to know.

**Nauthiz.** Meaning limits or limited, enduring, determination, or patience. This suggests that you might be encountering obstacles in your life and it's important to endure or to have patience. Although this might seem on the surface like a negative rune, it's actually telling you to not give up and see this through to the end. Additionally, it might suggest that you accept your own limitations.

**Inguz.** This rune means the family, home and hearth. Finding this in your circle suggests you have a strong love in your life or a solid base. It can also indicate that you are open to stronger familial or romantic ties and now is a good time to initiate a new relationship. If this appears facedown, you should take a closer look at your relationships as you may be blocked.

## CHAPTER TEN: Divination

ᛖ

**Ehwaz.** This rune means strength and reliability. To find this inside your circle suggests that you or those you have in your life are trustworthy. It also indicates that you should feel comfortable and confident in your decisions at this time in your life. To find this face down suggests that you should be cautious. There may be those within your life who cannot be trusted, or whose motives are hidden from your view.

**Algiz.** Meaning protection and spiritual connection, this rune suggests a closeness to your deity. It might indicate that you are traveling on a spiritual path or that you might soon obtain a deeper meaning of your higher self. If the rune is facedown, it might suggest that you are struggling against yourself.

## CHAPTER TEN: Divination

**Fehu**. This is associated with gain, prosperity, and success. It is considered lucky to have it come up inside your circle face up. However, if it appears face down it means that your finances or the stability of your routine may be in question or simply unknown. There may be factors yet undecided in divining this element of your life. If it appears outside your circle, there may be outside factors influencing your life that can drastically change things. This may be unchangeable, uncontrollable, or simply outside your purview.

**Wunjo.** This rune generally means happiness, though not necessarily passion. This suggests a general contentment with your own life, finding pleasure and joy in the things you have in your life. If you find this facedown inside your circle, it could indicate that you are feeling frustrated or blocked with some aspect of your life. It may also indicate, if found outside the circle, that there is someone directly influencing – positively or negatively – your personal happiness.

## CHAPTER TEN: Divination

**Jera.** This means fruitfulness and hard work. Jera represents the coming of your just rewards. What you have sown, you will reap now in your life. Should this be within your circle, it means that these rewards are near or present in your life. Outside the circle suggests that they may be a result of an outside force. Facedown indicates that, while you indeed deserve to receive these things, you might find it problematic to do so. There may be something blocking or hiding them from you.

**Kano.** Representative of creativity and imagination, this might also represent prophecy or having a vision. If it appears facedown, this vision might be important but either deliberately blocked or inaccessible.

## CHAPTER TEN: Divination

**Teiwaz.** This rune symbolizes authority, honor, and justice. Should you find this rune inside your circle, then you can anticipate a level of strength within your life. It can also be indicative of loyalty – your loyalty to others or others' loyalty to you – and possibly suggest that there might be hardship on the horizon, but you must face it with honor and lead the charge forward. Finding this facedown might suggest that you are struggling with a moral decision.

**Berkana.** Meaning new beginnings or rebirth, this rune suggests a positive change – or more likely, a renewal or second chance. If you've recently regretted an action or decision, seeing this rune suggests that you attempt to either make amends or let this past indiscretion go. There are always second chances and this rune represents yours. Should you find this facedown, prepare for a struggle towards what you need and what is being offered to you.

## CHAPTER TEN: Divination

**Eiwaz.** This rune means movement and teamwork. Seeing this within your circle means that you are building upon a solid foundation, but that foundation is not the root of a tree. Instead it is like the bed of a river. Solid and stable, but ever shifting. Remember to build with those you value and trust.

**Laguz.** Indicative of dreams, secrets, and the spirits, this rune means that you should pay closer attention to your dreams and the secrets they might reveal to you. Listen to your spirit guide and remain open to your intuition. Finding this rune facedown suggests that you are blocked on a spiritual level.

## CHAPTER TEN: Divination

**Hagalaz.** Meaning challenges or disasters, either of large or small proportion. If found within the circle, this might mean that you are set on a course to face a difficulty in your life. Facedown, this might mean that this challenge could blindside you or come out of seemingly nowhere. For this one especially, it's important to consider how the other runes are placed in regards to Hagalaz.

**Raido**. This is a representation of traveling or moving. Although not specifically change, it might mean a *temporary* change in your life. It implies a locational adjustment of some kind. If it's facedown within the circle, it might represent immobility or being stuck.

**Thurisaz.** This rune means change and flexibility. Thurisaz shows up when either change is coming or when you are encouraged to be flexible, ready for the unexpected or prepared to bend when normally you might stand rigid. Facedown might suggest that an unexpected change is arriving soon and outside the circle might suggest that change is inevitable and should not be fought.

**Dagaz.** Meaning transformation and understanding, this rune suggests that you are at a point where change is beneficial. You are ready to take the next step. It might also suggest that you have gained recent wisdom or that you have overcome a previous obstacle in your path.

**Isa.** Representative of either frustration or delays, Isa means that you must have patience. There may be delays in what you need in your life, but you cannot make these things come to you any faster without frustration and failure. So find your patience.

**Sowilo.** Meaning good health and success, this rune can also symbolize the arrival of positive changes in your life. If found within the circle, anticipate a shift in your life for the better or good things to be moving within your sphere. Should this piece be found facedown in your circle, your success or happiness might be in question.

# A CLOSING NOTE

Magic is both incredibly simple and unendingly complex. It is what you make of it. You are the key factor in your own practice and it's important to listen to what your instincts are telling you. No matter what you read here or anywhere else, it's up to you to decide what's right. If it doesn't feel like something that you should be doing, then don't do it. Because if it doesn't feel right, then it probably won't work for you anyway. The Wiccan tradition is about exploring the natural world, but also about finding our own balance within that world. It's the reason that there are so many different practices out there, traditions that grow out of what people need this religion to be.

In the end, there is only one absolute law that spans across all traditions: And ye harm none, do what ye will.

So long as you stick to that creed, you cannot go wrong. And remember, you are included in that. Do no harm to others, but do no harm to yourself either. Because you are important. You are part of this balance, part of this world. Be as good to yourself as you are to others.

# NOTES

# NOTES

## INDEX

**A**

Algiz 97
Allspice 50
Altars 42
An athame. 43
Ansuz 94

**B**

Basil 50
Bay leaves 51
bell. 43
Beltane 79
Berkana 100
Book of Shadows 87

**C**

Candle Magic 64
candles 67
Caraway 51
Casting a Circle 32
chalice 44
Cinnamon 51
Clove 51
Color connotations 65
Cooking 60
Coriander 52
coven 71
Creativity 37
Crystal 46
Crystal. 46
Cumin 52

**D**

Dagaz 103
deity 26
Dill 52
dish 45

**E**

Ehwaz 97
Eiwaz 101
Esbats 81

**F**

Feather 46
Fehu 98
Festivals 76
Fire 24
Flou 52

**G**

Garlic 52
Gebo 93
Ginger 53
Goddesses consort 26

**H**

Hagalaz 102
Hazelnut 55
Herbal Magic 50

**I**

Imbolc 78
Inguz 96
Isa 104

**J**

Jera 99

**K**

Kano 99

## L

Laguz 101
Lavender 55
Law of Three 22
Lilac 55
Lughnasadh 80

## M

Mabon 81
Magic 10
Maiden 26
Mannaz 93
Misconceptions 27
moon 86
Mustard 53

## N

Nauthiz 96
Nutmeg 53

## O

Ostara 79
Othila 94

## P

Parsley 53
pentacle 45
Pepper 53
Peppermint 54
Persecution of Witche 16
Perth 95
Potions 5, 62, 89
Protection 58

## R

Raido 102
Red Pepper 54
Rose 56

## S

Sabbats 76
Saffron 56
Sage 47, 54
Salem Witch Trials 18
Salt 54
Samhain. 76
Satchels 58
solitary practitioner 86
Sowilo 104
Specificity 36
Spellcraft 35
Spirit 23
Stone 47

## T

Teiwaz 100
The Elements 22
Thurisaz 103

## U

Uruz 95

## V

Valerian 56
Vanilla 55

## W

Wand 46
water 45
Water 24
Wiccan Rede 22
wind. 23
Wunjo 98

## Y

Yule 78

Made in the USA
Lexington, KY
14 March 2018